THE LADY AND THE LIGHTHOUSE

AND
OTHER STUFF

Written by Ian Macaulay

Written and Published by:

Ian Macaulay

Prestatyn

Denbighshire

Illustrations by Shirley Macaulay

Copyright

Ian Macaulay asserts the right to be
identified as the author of this work.
© 2020

ISBN No. 978-0-9556262-9-6

Printed by Fineline Print & Web, Ruthin LL15 1HW (2020)

Having moved from Manchester to Talacre in 1972 the thought of leaving my friends and regular visits to Old Trafford was a difficult one to bear, but I soon realised that Talacre was a unique place to live. A close community, the sea beyond the sand hills and the arcades and fun fair atmosphere was a teenagers paradise, and living in a chip shop was an added bonus.

Living in Talacre inspired me to start writing and I hope you enjoy reading this book as much as I did writing and reminiscing.

Thank you to my daughters, Claire and Michelle, for their
inspiration and their belief in me.

To Shirley, my Mum, for all her illustrations and her
motivation and help in producing this book.

Jeff Nicholson for his advice and support.

Gordon Jones from Colwyn Bay -
sadly missed but still respected.

For my grandchildren, Olivia, Jack and Ruby.

Stay forever young, old age is just for the elderly.

CONTENTS

Pg.

CONTENTS

MEMORIES OF TALACRE

While visiting Talacre
Oh how the time has flown
Houses that I used to know
Are sand dunes overgrown

As I strolled along the Warren
No shacks, all families gone
No more happy faces
Of children having fun

I stopped a while and rested
On a quiet piece of land
In front of me an empty space
Where the bakery used to stand

For those that now reside here
Please listen to the tales
And pass them on to people new
Of Talacre in North Wales

As I started walking to my car
I turned my head to see
A different kind of Warren
From how it used to be

Our childhoods should be happy days
It certainly was for me
My heart will stay forever
In Talacre by the sea.

Ian Macaulay

THE LADY AND THE LIGHTHOUSE

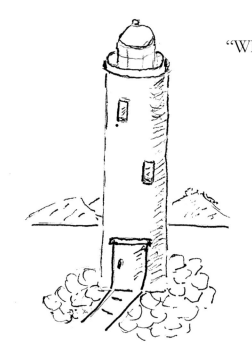

"I know" said Olivia

"When we've had our tea and toast"

"Let's go down to Talacre

And find the lighthouse ghost

.

They say she is a lady

Who wears a dress of white.

But people only see her

When the church bells strike at night."

"I'm not sure " said Ruby,

With her brown eyes open wide.

"Just hold Livvy's hand " said Jack,

"I'll hold the other side."

So Livvy, Jack and Ruby

Tiptoed gently through the night

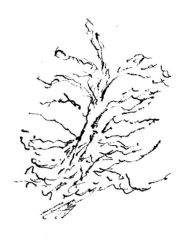

Heading for Talacre

And the lady dressed in white.

It took them quite a while

Walking through the whispering sand

With Jack and Ruby either side

Holding Livvy's hand.

Then there it was, in front of them

Looking out to sea,

The lighthouse of Talacre

Stood proud for all to see.

"Let's go inside" said Livvy,

Stay close we'll be alright

And maybe if we're lucky

We'll see the ghost to-night."

The door was brown and rusty

From the crashing of the sea

Then underneath a loosened rock

They found an old, worn key.

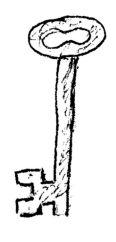

Liv put the key inside thelock

And turned it to the right.

They gave the door a mighty kick,

Which gave them all a fright.

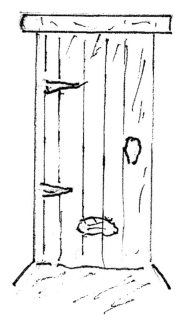

The door eased open gently

With a groan, as if in pain.

They stepped inside

From the cold, dark night

And sheltered from the rain.

" Turn the light on," Ruby said.

"There is n't one," said Jack.

"Why's it called theLighthouse then

I'm scared,

I'm going back."

"Hold my hand," said Livvy,

"It's going to be allright,

We'll huddle close together

And hold each other tight."

"This doesn't feel like fun to me,"

Said Jack, "I want my Mum."

As they huddled close together,

That's the end of chapter one.

So chapter two has just begun

With them huddled in the night

All thinking of the lady

Who wears a dress of white.

"Let's climb the stairs," said Livvy

"Try not to make a sound.

It looks like these are special stairs,

They take us round and round."

It seemed they climbed forever

Till they couldn't climb no more.

At last they reached a resting place

With an old, green wooden door.

Above the door there hung a sign

To the left there hung a clock.

The sign said - Tell the time for me,

And give the door a knock.

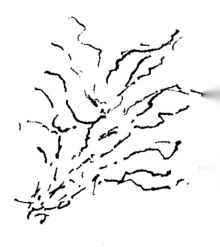

So Livvy read the time

And tapped upon the door.

With their eyes and mouths wide open

They heard footsteps on the floor.

The door squeaked open gently

And stood there was a man.

He puffed ~~his pipe and~~ smiled

And said "Hello, I'm Captain Stan."

"Did you read the sign above the door

And did you read the time?

I need to know what time it is

Then more steps there are to climb.

Have you come to see the lady,

The lady dressed in white?

I need to know the time," he said

"The timing must be right."

"It's ten past ten," said Livvy

"Now what do we do?"

"Remember that my door is green,"
Said Stan, "Now that's a clue.

You need to solve the riddle
Before the end of night,

And then you'll have the password
To see my friend in white."

He smiled at them and closed the door
And waved them on their way,

And reminded them to solve the riddle
Before the break of day.

The three of them went on their way

To climb another flight.

They knew that time was running out

Before they saw daylight.

"Remember that green door," said Livvy

"He said it was a clue."

So there we leave them, climbing stairs

That's the end of chapter two.

So chapter three's upon us,

And they've collected their first clue

They're heading further up the stairs

For the door, their second clue.

Ruby said "I'm tired now,"

And Jack said, "So am I.

How longer do we have to climb,

We must have reached the sky."

"Just another one or two,"

Said Livvy with a smile.

When we've reached the second door

We can rest there for a while."

Then, there it was, a yellow door.

The three all stood outside.

On the wall was hung a rusty bell

With an arrow by its side.

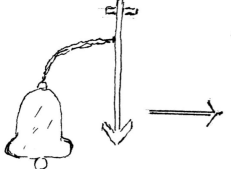

The sign above said - Ring me,

Then ring again once more,

Then give a gentle tap

On the little yellow door.

They gave the bell a little ring,

Then rang it once again.

The door then slowly opened

By a man called sailor Kane.

"I'm Kane," he said, "Hello you three.

What brings you here to-night?

Are you looking for the lady

Who dresses all in white."

The three of them looked up at him

And nodded their three heads.

He said, "It's rather late m'dears,

You should be in your beds."

"I know," said Jack and Ruby,

And Livvy said, "Me too,

But we've been told to come and see you

To collect our second clue."

So sailor Kane looked down at Jack,

He said, "Listen, little fellow,

Remember that my wooden door

Is painted in bright yellow."

"So now be on your way, my friends,
And don't look back at me.

Time is running out for you.
It's almost ten to three,

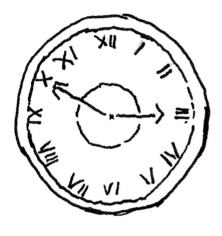

And time is of the essence, child,
Make haste, be on your way.

You ~~need~~ to find the lady
~~Before the break~~ of day."

"Come on ," said Livvy, "Hold my hand,"
To Ruby and to Jack.

"Remember what the sailor said,
We must not dare look back."

So there we leave them, holding hands,
As tight as tight can be.

That brings us to the end, my friends
Of chapter number three.

As chapter four begins

They're still walking round and round.

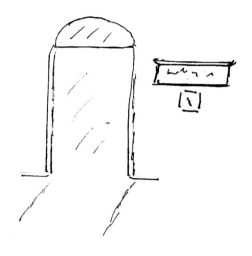

With every single step they take

They're further from the ground.

It seemed they climbed forever,

And then they climbed some more.

Still searching for their final clue

Another wooden door.

Eventually they find a space

Where an old door used to be

With a switch and a sign above it

Saying - Switch me on to see.

So Livvy reached and clicked the switch.

She kept clicking to and fro.

"I doesn't work," they heard a voice,

" It broke some years ago."

'Come in," he said, "and I'm right here,
There's something I should say

You're late, I've been expecting you
Since half past yesterday

"Half past yesterday," said Jack,
"I don't know what you mean."

"Well yesterday's a place, young man,
Where everybody's been.

And to-morrow is a place
Where no-ones ever gone,

And to-days a place you'll always be
Until the day is done

"Now, listen very carefully
And things will be allright.

I know the reason that you're here -
To see my friend in white.

My name is Captain Roly,
I used to sail the sea,

And now I keep a lookout
For castaways like me.

There used to be a big, bright light
Slowly spinning round,

To warn the ships of danger
And steer clear of rocky ground.

My friend who I look out for
Each dark and lonely night,

Is the husband of a friend of mine,
The lady dressed in white."

"He sailed away to sea

A long, long time ago

We've never seen him since that day.

What happened, we don't know.

I made a promise to my friend

I'd keep a lookout every night.

His wife would walk along the dunes

In a flowing dress of white.

And just in case I fell asleep

And missed him coming back,

She said she'd only dress in white

And never dress in black.

"So through the dunes she walks alone,
Only dressed in white,

For him to recognise her
As she waits for him at night.

The little wooden door you saw,
I painted that one green,

To remind him of the sand dunes
Where he'd met her as a 'teen.

The other I painted yellow,
To remind him of the sun,

And the times they spent together
Holding hands and having fun.

The room in which you're standing,
You'll notice there's no door,

It's a symbol that the lady's love
Stays open evermore."

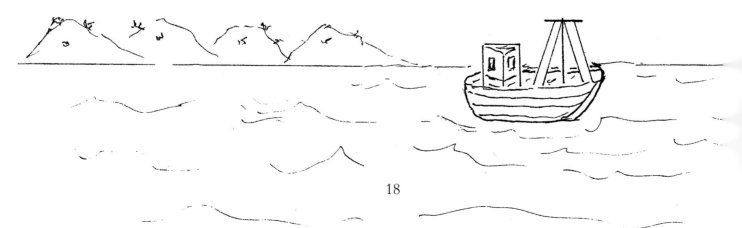

So Livvy, Jack and Ruby

Stared at the open door.

At the space of where it should have been.

That's the end of chapter four.

So chapter five's upon us

As they race against the night,

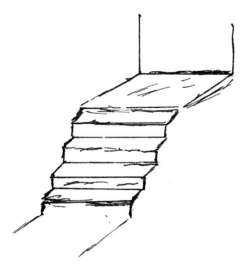

To find the mystery lady

Who wears a dress of white.

"Now follow me," the Captain said,

As they all rose from their chairs.

"We need to get a move on,

So follow me downstairs."

The stairs they found so hard to climb,

Seemed easier going down.

They stayed behind the Captain,

And finally reached the ground.

They'd left the rusty, lighthouse door

Ajar, without a care.

As Captain Roly pushed it hard,

They smelt the salt, sea air.

The sea was getting closer,
Rolling in to shore

As they heard the hollow clanging
Of the rusty lighthouse door.

They needed to take shelter
So they hid behind a dune.

The four gazed up to the starlit sky
And the silvery full moon.

He said"Now stand together
And look towards my right."

And there just in the distance
Was a lady, dressed in white.

Olivia, Jack and Ruby held each other tight
As the figure got much closer, the lady dressed in white.

"Don't be afraid," the Captain said,
Brushing down his coat.

Ruby said,"She walks like us.
I thought a ghost would float."

The lady smiled and looked at them
With beautiful, blue eyes.

Her lacy dress, fluorescent white
Lit up the darkened skies.

Her skin was just like porcelain,
Her hair as soft as snow.

She told them that she walked the dunes
With nowhere else to go.

22

Then said, "To some the sea looks calm

And friendly as can be.

But it took my man away from me.

Now I'm lonely as you see.

So each night I walk and wait a while

So lonely and so weak."

She looked into the childrens eyes

As a tear ran down her cheek.

"Please, never be afraid of me,

I don't mean any harm.

And never think the sea is safe

Because it looks so calm.

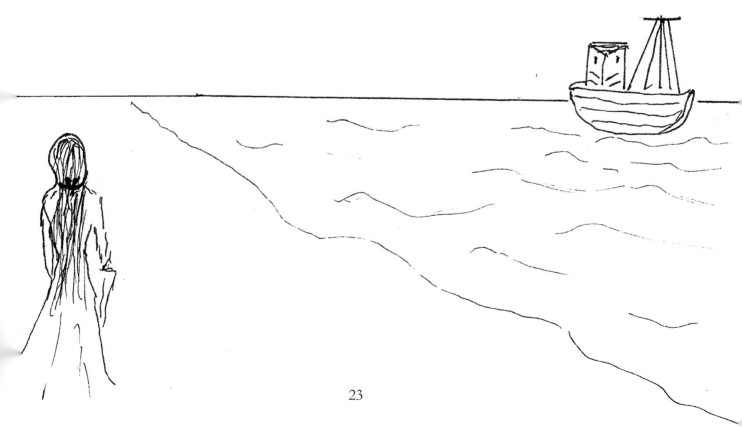

"It took my love away from me,

I've been alone for years.

I only ever walk at night

To hide my constant tears.

So thank you for your time tonight,

Ruby, Jack and Liv,

To show I really mean it

I've a gift I'd like to give.

I always carry with me

Three little, silver fish.

Put them in your pockets.

Each one will grant a wish.

"Be careful what you wish for,

The wishes will come true.

Think a while before you wish,

Be aware of what you do.

So now I must go on my way,

And keep walking all alone.

I need to keep a lookout

For my sweetheart, coming home."

The moon went down, the sun came up.

It was the break of day.

The lady in white had vanished,

And the Captain went away.

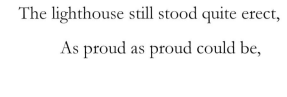

The lighthouse still stood quite erect,
As proud as proud could be,

Amongst the whisper of the sand
And the glitter off the sea.

"Where have they gone?" said Ruby.
"I don't know," said Jack.

"Hold my hands," said Livvy,
"It's time we headed back."

As they walked and left the lighthouse,
Still standing proud, alone,

They turned their heads, and all held hands
As they headed back for home.

"Hang on," said Jack, "We've all forgot.
What about our fish?

We've got them in our pockets
And she said to make a wish."

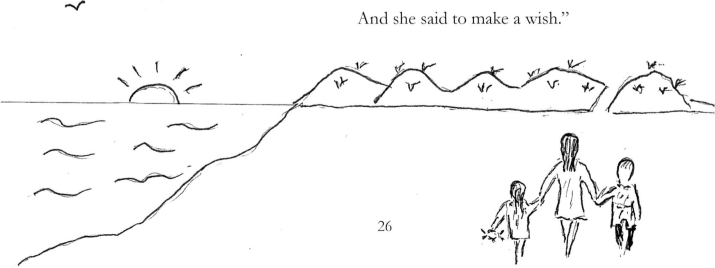

"I know just what I'll wish for,"

said Ruby with a smile.

I'll wish for that big light to work,

And shine out for a mile.

So all the ships can see the light,

And no-ones lost at sea,

And all the sailors on their ships

Can get back home for tea."

Livvy said,"I'll go next

To make a special wish."

As she went into her pocket,

She held the silver fish.

"I wish the special lady
Could be happy, just like me,

And never feel alone
As she's looking out to sea.

And the sailors who go sailing
Upon the waves of foam,

Are never lost at sea,
And return safely to their home."

Then Jack felt in his pocket,
And held his fish so tight,

And knew he'd never be afraid
Of ghosts, in bed at night.

And wished he'd see the lady,
Walking hand in hand,

Reunited with her sweetheart
Along the golden sand.

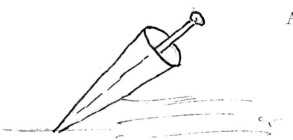

So there they were, back at home,

Eating tea and toast.

Speaking of their adventure,

And the bits they liked the most.

Then just as they were thinking

It could have been a dream,

Flashing past their window

Appeared a golden beam.

"They've fixed the light," said Ruby,

"Our wishes have come true,

It's lighting up the silver sand

And the glistening sea of blue."

Then as the beam came back around,

Lighting up the sand,

It shone upon a couple,

Walking hand in hand.

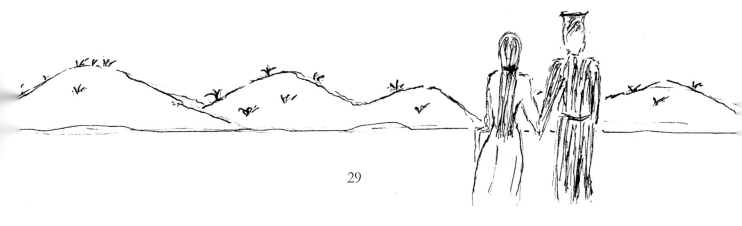

The lady, she was dressed in white,
The man was dressed in black.

As they walked along together,
The ladys head turned back.

Her face was still like porcelain.
Her eyes were still so blue.

Her cherry lips said "Thank you"
To the children she now knew.

The children waved and smiled at her
As she walked along the coast.

Their adventure now completed
They enjoyed their tea and toast.

THE END

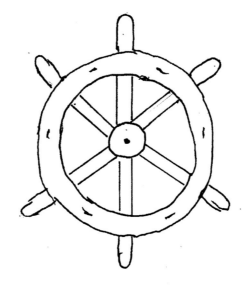

THE HISTORY OF TALACRE LIGHTHOUSE

As the sun sets and the sea sweeps in across Talacre beach the lighthouse often seems to float on the waves. It is a mysterious and beautiful optical illusion that attracts visitors from all across Britain. Correctly known as "Point of Ayr" lighthouse, it was originally built in 1776 by a trust of the Mayor, Recorder and Aldermen of Chester to help guide ships away from the nearby sandbanks and provide a bearing for the great port of Liverpool to the north east and mark the Mersey and the Dee.

Unusually for a lighthouse, the tower was actually built on the beach. Around 1818 the original building was destroyed by the sea and in 1820 it was taken over by Trinity House and a more robust tower was erected in its place. This is the building still standing today.

It is around 60 feet tall, 18 feet in diameter and has oak pile foundations and originally featured two lights. One was directed at shipping out to sea, whilst the second beam illuminated the mouth of the river Dee. After being replaced by an ocean based metal -pile lighthouse the Talacre tower was decommissioned between 1883 and 1884 over the years it slowly fell into disrepair.

In 2010 a stainless steel figure - the keeper - was erected on the balcony as an artistic project mutually agreed by the then owner and the Flintshire County Council. In 2011 the landmark was offered for sale.

Talacre lighthouse has been featured in both television programmes and adverts. It is most well known as the lighthouse in the Dulux paint advert. The Point of Ayr, Y parlwr du in Welsh, is the northern most point of mainland Wales and is located 540 yards to the north of the Talacre Beach Caravan Park. It can also be accessed from Station Road to the East. The dunes surrounding Talacre lighthouse are recognised as having a special scientific interest as they are inhabited by a precious collection of natterjack toads.

MOUNT PLEASANT RESCUE

The night of October 6-7 went on record as a very stormy one. A hurricane blew in from the north-west making extremely dangerous conditions in Liverpool bay. That night, which was a Sunday, a Norwegian freighter was trying to reach the safety of the River Mersey, having made the Atlantic crossing from Quebec. The freighter was called the Mount Pleasant and the masters name was Skipper Pedersen. In order to negotiate the entrance channel into the Mersey, the freighter had to be taken in tow with the sails furled. Around midnight the towing gear broke and such was the force of the hurricane the Mount Pleasant was driven away from the Mersey to the coast of north-east Wales. Due to the presence of sandbanks this was a particularly dangerous part of the coast, the most dreaded being the West Hoyle Bank.

▲ Copy of Medal from October 7th 1889 presented to Mr. Williams Roberts who was only 15 at the time of the rescue.

Just before noon on October 7 the crew, who came from Kristiania in Norway, were clinging on for dear life as they watched the breakers that they would soon be in the midst of. Then they were in blinding spray with huge waves crashing down onto their now grounded vessel and battering them mercilessly.

The founding of the ship had been seen from the shore and three lifeboats set out to try to reach the wreck. In one of these lifeboats, which had 12 crew and was a rowing boat, was a 15 year old boy called William Roberts who had volunteered to help the rescue.

As they approached the Mount Pleasant, the crew threw overboard lifebuoys with lines attached. These drifted within reach of the lifeboat men who hauled them aboard and contact was made between the two vessels. Next a hawser was attached to the lines and by thus means each member of the crew of the Mount Pleasant was hauled to safety. Later they were transferred to the tug boat from Liverpool and taken to await passage home to Kristiania.

Skipper Pederson said the crew were constantly in danger of their lives and the Norwegian Consul General sent a recommendation to the Norwegian Government that the bravery of the Gronant men, who were all volunteers, should be recognised.

Some weeks later a moving ceremony was held at the National School in Ffynnongroew, where Lord Mostyn, acting on behalf of King Oscar of Norway, presented each of the men with a silver medal.

◄ **Mr. William Roberts**

(my Great Grandfather in his later life)

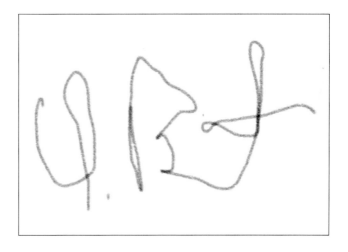

▲ **The signature of**

Mr. William Roberts

MOST MYSTERIOUS

Talacre "Point of Ayr" lighthouse is definitely haunted!

That is the belief of many hundreds of people who have visited it over the decades.

People who live nearby claim to have seen ghostly lights and a lady dressed in white walking along the pathway which the local people call the cob, and there are many accounts of dogs refusing to go near the lighthouse, and whining in fear if brought too close by their owners. Visitors to the tower often reported that they felt a threatening presence and many claim to have felt nauseous while inside.

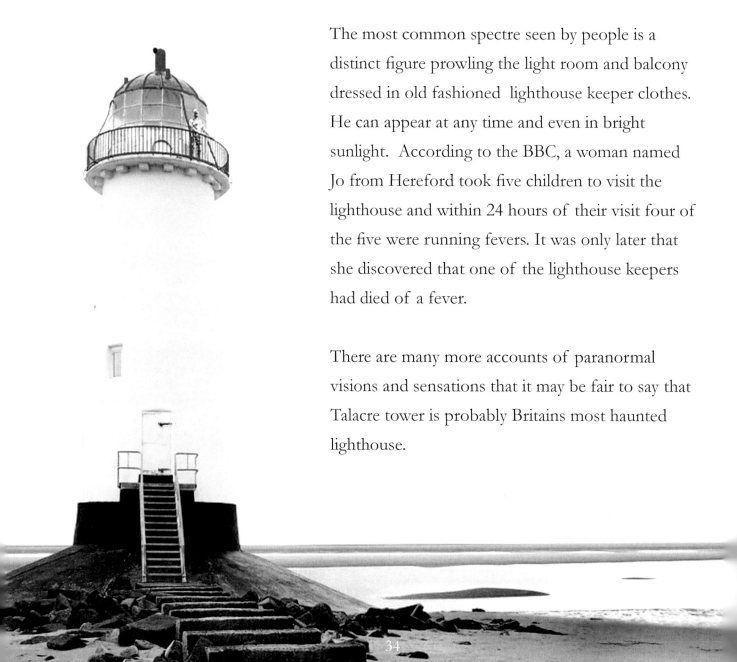

The most common spectre seen by people is a distinct figure prowling the light room and balcony dressed in old fashioned lighthouse keeper clothes. He can appear at any time and even in bright sunlight. According to the BBC, a woman named Jo from Hereford took five children to visit the lighthouse and within 24 hours of their visit four of the five were running fevers. It was only later that she discovered that one of the lighthouse keepers had died of a fever.

There are many more accounts of paranormal visions and sensations that it may be fair to say that Talacre tower is probably Britains most haunted lighthouse.

FACTS OF TALACRE LIGHTHOUSE

1. Talacre Lighthouse is the oldest lighthouse in all of Wales.

2. It is as old as the independent incarnation of America (the signing of the Declaration of Independence)

3. No longer functioning the site had a working lighthouse for approximately 70 years.

4. The lighthouse is among one of the more haunted locations in the whole of the United Kingdom.

5. There are many reports of paranormal activity and sightings of ghostly apparitions inside the tower standing today.

6. The lighthouse has a 7 foot tall statue of the lighthouse keeper that honours his memory.

7. The figure is a stainless steel sculpture by the formidable artist Angela Smith.

8. The beach around the lighthouse is now a nature reserve.

9. The lighthouse is a grade ll listed building.

10. From the lighthouse there are views across the river Dee estuary to the Wirral and on a clear day you can see the Blackpool coastline.

11. The lighthouse was featured in the background of a 2011 television advertisement by the paint manufacturer Dulux. The advertisement was designed to mark the 50th anniversary of the first appearance of the Old English Sheepdog mascot.

NORMAN

Norman was a donkey
Of which you can't deny
But Norman wasn't handsome
He had a wonky eye

The other donkeys thought it good
To laugh at Norman's look
But Norman didn't mind at all
He thought he was a duck

"Let them laugh" said Norman
"I'm happy with my looks"
And trotted down the farmyard
To swim with all the ducks

The ducks befriended Norman
They treated him as one
They knew an ugly duckling
Could turn into a swan

So next time you see a donkey
Have a closer look
It could be poor old Norman
Who thinks he is a duck

A BUNGALOW BY THE SEA

Now Jeremy was very tall
As tall as tall can be
He lived in a tiny bungalow
Which overlooked the sea

Now this was rather odd we know
But Jeremy was pleased
He had a hole made in the roof
For access to the trees

You only usually see giraffes
When visiting the zoo
Or going on safari
There're more than one or two

But Jeremy was different
You'd hear his neighbours cry
"Hey, Jeremy, what's the weather like
You're nearest to the sky?"

Jeremy would laugh and say
"I think it looks like snow"
He was very very happy
In his little bungalow

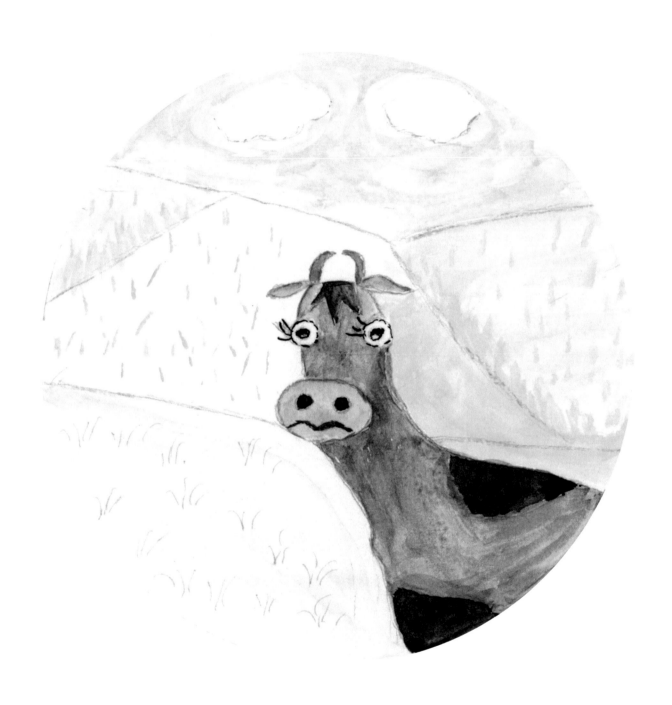

BORED BELLA

"Oh, why is my life so boring
Will another hour pass
So slowly, stood out in a field
Just eating soggy grass?

To be a cow is not so good"
Said Bella with a sigh
"All I've got to look at
Is grass and trees and sky

"I'd rather be a sheepdog
At least he goes to town
And I'm just stuck in this big field
Oh, I think I'll just lie down

I'm not really one for moaning
But another day has gone
As I look into the next big field
Where they seem to have such fun

So I'll stay here lying down
In my field but won't complain
At least you know when a cow lies down
It's probably going to rain"

PETER PIG

"I don't like the mud" said Peter Pig
"Why can't we be clean?
Rolling around in mud all day
It's really not my scene.

I know it doesn't sound quite right
For a pig who likes to wash
My piggy friends don't talk to me
They think I'm rather posh!

Just because they like the mud
They just don't understand
When I stroll round the farmyard
Looking rather grand.

Well it's dinner time
I'm going now to eat my apple pie
I'll leave the rest to make a mess
In their muddy little sty."

THE FISH WHO COULDN'T SWIM

Heres a little story
About a fish called Jim
He wasn't like the other fish
Jimmy couldn't swim

So he thought he'd ride a bicycle
And cycle under sea
But Jim kept falling off it
He had no hands you see

He tried to use a pogo stick
And landed with a bump
He forgot he needed legs for that
And Jimmy couldn't jump

He thought it best to try no more
He wasn't one to fuss
So he lay down on the sea bed
And waited for a bus

THE BOY AND THE SHARK

I met a shark when I went for a swim

He looked at me and I looked at him

He had small eyes and big white teeth

His body was grey and white underneath

I said, "Hello" he said "Hello " back

He had a big fin stuck on his back

He said "Hold on to my tail and we'll go for a swim"

So I held on tight and went swimming with him

He took me to places where only sharks know

Deep under the sea where people don't go

I saw lots of fish and an old shipwreck too

Octopus, turtles and a dolphin he knew

Then we went to the top through waves full of foam

It was time for my tea and I had to go home

As I held his tail we headed for shore

I wasn't frightened of sharks anymore

He said "Goodbye", I said "Goodbye " to him

I gave him a wave and said "Thanks for the swim"

My mum came towards me ,"Where have you been?"

She said, sounding worried, making a scene

I said I'd been swimming under the sea

She said "Don't be silly, let's go home and have tea"

PIRATE STAN

There once was a man called Pirate Stan
Who sailed in boat on the sea
He took great pleasure searching for treasure
With a parrot on his shoulder called Flea

They'd sail over the ocean,
Or so the stories told
Looking for diamonds, jewels and pearls
And a treasure chest full of gold

He lived on an island hidden away
Where no-one else could see
Just Pirate Stan with a patch on his eye
And a parrot on his shoulder called Flea

His house was small with a little wooden wall
Where he would sit and polish his gun
He'd eat bread and honey as he counted his money
In the early morning sun

Then he'd set sail on a treasure trail
To see what he could see
To look for things like diamond rings
With a parrot on his shoulder called Flea

Now Pirate Stan was a greedy man
And his boat sank to the bottom of the sea
So that was the end of Pirate Stan
And his parrot on his shoulder called Flea

But late at night when the moon shines bright
If you listen carefully
You'll hear the cry of a man with one eye
And a squawk from his parrot called Flea

MATCH OF THE DAY

"Fancy a kickabout Grandad"
Said a voice outside the door
"I think I'll be Ronaldo,
You be Dennis Law"

"Okay" I said "Give me the ball
Yes I know it's immature
But so is a sixty one year old
Who thinks he's Denis Law

So off I kicked and straightaway
The ball was in my grasp
As Ronaldo tapped my ankles
I gave the ball a blast

It rebounded off the garden bench
And hit the windowsill
Ronaldo heads towards the goal
And there it was, one - nil

He volleyed in the second
Then scored another four
As he started to humiliate
The legend Denis Law

So as I left the garden
As he dribbled round some cones
I saw a future "Busby Babe"
In my Grandson young Jack Jones

DAD'S BIRTHDAY

Helping mum to bake a cake
Is so much fun for me
She lets me climb upon a chair
To see what I can see

She rolls my sleeves up very high
So I don't make a mess
'Cos underneath my apron
Is my favourite party dress

We're making Dad a birthday cake
As a very big surprise
He says he's twenty one again
But Mum says he tells lies

Mummy lets me lick the bowl
Which I find so much fun
She says that I'm a real big help
'Cos the washing up's all done

The cake goes in the oven
Which Mummy does for me
That's a job for grown-ups
Not little girls of three

I love to help my Mum bake cakes
What a lovely time I've had
I hope he'll like this special cake
HAPPY BIRTHDAY, DAD!

GROWING UP

I woke up on Monday and opened my eyes
Something felt different, but to my surprise
I looked in the mirror and what did I see
A big yellow spot staring at me
When I peeked through my fingers my blood ran cold
'Cos I'm just a girl of eleven years old

Where did it come from while I was in bed
A big yellow spot at the front of my head
Mum told me spots won't happen at night
I always believed her then turned on the light

What do I do, it's Monday, its school
My friends will all laugh, I'll look such a fool
Don't be so silly I heard my Mum say
It's only a spot it'll soon go away

You don't understand I said in reply
It's a big yellow spot, it's like a third eye
She said Don't be daft and be on your way
Remember your homework and have a nice day
So I slammed the front door and walked down the street
Hood up, head down, dragging my feet

Now a secret I'd kept as eleven year olds do
I fancied a boy, Sam, in year two
He's gorgeous, he's clever, friends he has lots
And I've got to face him with a big yellow spot

So I sat down in lesson and pulled down my hood
Glanced round the classroom not feeling too good
Sam came in late and sat next to me
His eyes were all red, he'd been crying like me

I said to him, Sam, whatever's to do
He took off his cap and he had one too
We started to laugh, that cheered us both up
I guess this is life when a girl's growing up

OUR OLIVIA

Now Livvi you're a teenager
The years have passed us by
You've turned into a lady
The apple of our eye

Thirteen years of love and joy
You bring to all that's near
You laughter, love and friendship
We treasure oh so dear

The love we hold and share for you
We think that you should know
We'll hold forever in our hearts
And never let it go

So this is just to tell you
How much you're truly loved
Not only by the family here
But the family up above

Who are always looking down on you
Each and every day
And whisper that they love you
In their private special way

So as you go through life our Liv
Keep smiling all the way
And make sure that you remember
You're treasured every day

BLACKPOOL

Let's all go to Blackpool my Dad said with a smile
I'll take you on the donkeys then walk the golden mile
We'll stay in bed and breakfast that overlooks the sea
Toffee apples for breakfast and candy floss for tea
I really was excited, Are we nearly there
I'd ask as we left our street and talked about the fair

It seemed to take forever travelling in the car
Thinking of the Tower and the Merry England bar
We'd always go and see a show at the end of every pier
North , South and Central where Dad would have a beer
We'd jump on trams and then get off and jump back on again
Oh what fun I had in Blackool, a girl of only ten

Now nothing lasts forever, or so some people say
But my happy childhood memories will never fade away
Now years have gone and times moved on, I'm a Mum now and a wife
But never will forget those days the happiest of my life

So now I take my children to Blackpool every year
To show them all the things I did and where Dad had a beer
I hope they'll remember Blackpool and have lots of fun like me
Where I had toffee apples and candy floss for tea.

THE HOLE IN THE FENCE

A fox comes in my garden
When I'm in bed at night
He gets in through a little hole
In the fence just to the right

He has a little look around
To see what he can find
While I'm standing on my tiptoes
Peeping through the blind

There's nothing in my garden
To interest Mr Fox
Just Dad's old bike and a watering can
And an empty cardboard box

So he turns around and slips away
Escaping in the night
Squeezing through the hole again
In the fence just to the right

I never saw the fox again
Whilst in bed at night
Because Dad had fixed the hole up
In the fence just to the right

DREAMING

Where do we go to at night
He said as Mum turned out the light
Does she have a peep
While I'm fast asleep
Just to see if things are alright

Where do we go in our dreams
To a nice peaceful, place so it seems
There is always a space
In this wonderful place
Where the light grows stronger and beams

I can fight with some pirates, on the high seas
And play with their ill-gotten treasure
Give them the slip
And take over their ship
And sail it away at my leisure

The morning has come and I hear my Mum
Turn the handle of my bedroom door
She leans over the bed
And kisses my head
And tiptoes away as I snore

Now I'll always know where we all go
At night when she turns out the light
Your Mum has a peep
To see we're asleep
As dreaming of pirates we'll fight.

THINGS I KNOW

I know a goat that lived on a boat
Who sailed out to sea
He leaves the shore at half past four
And he's back in time for tea

I know a snail that left a trail
As he crawled along so slow
Rain or shine he leaves a trail of slime
Everywhere he goes

Have you heard, I know a bird
Who flies so high in the sky
He lands in a tree and sings to me
As the clouds go floating by

I know a dog that sleeps on a log
In a meadow by a stream
He sleeps all day in a field of hay
And makes a funny noise when he dreams

I know a fish that made a wish
And the wish he made came true
He wished that he could swim in a sea
In a beautiful colour of blue

So these were some of the things he knew
A little boy of three
Who thinks of them quite often
Because that little boy was me

BEDTIME

Lay down little Ruby

And rest your sweet head

It's been a long day and it's time for your bed

To dream about Tigger

And Winnie the Pooh

Eeyore and Piglet

Kanga and Roo

To dream about things

That make you laugh

Like Mummy and Daddy and foam in the bath

Chocolate and Wotsits

And nice things to eat

Cuddles and kisses

And tickles on feet

In the morning you'll wake

With a beautiful smile

And think of the things you dreamt for a while

People you met

And places you've been

Things that you did

When asleep, Ruby Jean

So lay down little Ruby

And rest your sweet head

It's been a long day and it's time for your bed

MR MOUSE

When I was very little
I had a little mouse
I kept him in a matchbox
In my bedroom in my house

I didn't call him anything
'Cos he didn't have a name
I just kept him in a matchbox
But loved him all the same

When I went to bed at night
I let him out to play
I forgot to close my window
And mouse just ran away

I think he lives up in the field
Opposite my house
I guess living in a matchbox
Wasn't home for Mr Mouse

So now I shut my window
And make sure it's always locked
But never will forget my friend
That lived in a little box

ROBIN REDBREAST

There's a little robin redbreast
Who visits every year
It's usually at Christmas time
On my fence he just appears

You'll see him on a Christmas card
On a post box full of snow
But never in the Summer time
I wonder where he goes

Does he fly to other places
To get warm and take a rest
Or simply goes back to the hedge
And settles in his nest

So if you see a robin
This Christmas when it snows
Watch him as he flies away
And tell me where he goes

THE NAUGHTY MONKEY

"Oh, look at them" the lady said
Peering through the cage
"They've always been my favourite
Since a very early age"

But monkey didn't like the way
The people all made fun
And hurled a well aimed missile
A half eaten fresh cream bun

It hit the ladys glasses
She gave a mighty scream
Her glasses fell and hit the ground
And covered her in cream

"You naughty little monkey
The creams gone in my eye"
But monkey wasn't finished yet
And hit her with a pie

The lady picked her glasses up
She stormed off in a rage
And never took the time again
To look through monkey's cage

THE BADGER AND THE OWL

Bobby is a badger
His face is black and white
He sleeps all through the daytime
And plays all through the night

Now Bobby's got a special friend
They call him Twit to Woo
He sits up high and looks around
To see what people do

Bobby goes out walking
To have a wander round
And signals to his friend above
To swoop down to the ground

They play a game of hide and seek
While everyone's in bed
Until the moon goes down again
And the sun breaks fiery red

You won't see them play at night
You'll be fast asleep
But if you're not and see them
It's a secret you should keep

FARMER NED

Early in the morning
Before the break of dawn
Farmer Ned gets out of bed
And puts his wellies on

He hurries down the farmyard
And unlocks the metal gate
Then spashed his way across the field
Worried he'll be late

Ned would feed his animals
To make them big and strong
Pigs and sheep and baby lambs
It didn't take him long

His last stop was the dairy
The job he loved the most
He'd milk the cow and the milk went home
For breakfast tea and toast

Then when he'd had his breakfast
At precisely half past ten
Back went on his wellingtons
To do it all again

THE FARMYARD

As snowflakes fall on the farmyard
On a cold December night
The sky is grey at the end of the day
And the fields a sea of white

All our friends are sleeping
There's not a single sound
To be heard amongst the animals
No footprints on the ground

Farmer Ned is in his bed
Quietly whistling while asleep
The snow outside is gathering
And getting fairly deep

Peter Pig is snuggled up
And Norman's on his hay
Monkey's snoring in his cage
Tomorrow's Christmas Day

The silence only broken
By a banging old barn door
And Farmer Ned who's sound asleep
Lets out a gentle snore

The special star up in the sky
Is shining oh so bright
From all our friends in the farmyard

MERRY CHRISTMAS AND GOODNIGHT!

SOMEONE'S SHUT THE CHIPPY DOWN

Someone's shut the chippy down, I heard Mum on the phone
I couldn't quite believe my eyes, she said to Aunty Joan
He's home at six, it's Friday night, whatever will I do
Joan said, very calmy, Don't panic, make a stew

A stew, she said, it's Friday, I don't think he'll agree
He always has his pie and peas on Friday for his tea
Mum came off the phone to Joan and sat down in her chair
She put her hands up to her head, ran her fingers through her hair

The clock struck six, the door banged shut, and then appeared my Dad
I'm home, he said, Hello, she said, Good day, Aye , not bad
Off came his coat, he hung it up behind the kitchen door
Sat down with his paper at the table set for four

Mum said, Now love, please don't shout, what I have to say is true
Someone's shut the chippy down so I've made a lovely stew
A stew, he said, it's Friday night, where's my peas and pie
With knife and fork clenched in his fists and anger in his eye

I'm not eating stew, we're going out for tea
He put his coat back on again and shouted, Follow me
So we all went out and had our pies and Dad had stopped his moan
Mum put the stew back in the pan and gave it to Aunty Joan.

FIRST AND LAST ATTEMPT

I've planted my seeds for the summer
Tomatoes and peppers galore
I talk to them every morning
Behind the greenhouse door

But nothing seems to be happening
Three weeks have come and gone
There's still not a single sprout appeared
Looks like they need more sun

So I've moved them in the direction
Of the burning summer sun
I've talked to them and watered them
But still nothing, not a one

I've taken advice from gardeners
And all those green fingered men
Still not a thing is sprouting
So I've moved them around again

Six weeks have passed and still no joy
No movement in any way
So I've put them back in the greenhouse
And that's where they're going to stay

So if you're thinking of growing tomatoes
Or peppers or onions or leeks
Go and buy them from Tesco
And save yourself six weeks.

THE CHRISTMAS LIST

I'm writing out my Christmas list To send to you know who!
I don't know why I'm bothered, I'm nearly eighty two.

I'm not asking for a bike or toys
For an Xbox I don't care.
I'm asking him for hair dye
To hide my greying hair

I'm not interested in Rudolph
Or what's in Santa's sack
Just an orthopaedic shoe
And a cushion for my back

The kissing by the mistletoe
Are distant memories
It takes me all my time these days
To rise from bended knees

No more hanky panky,
I never was a fan,
My time's spent in the kitchen
Making strawberry jam

I'm asking for a stairlift
Or a walking stick will do
That matches with my cushion
And my orthopaedic shoe

I'm well aware that Santa
Visits once a year
He can make a lot of noise - that's fine,
I'm deaf in my left ear

So he wouldn't wake me up you see
Even if he's late
I go to bed quite early
I'm asleep for half past eight

So that's my Christmas list all done, to send to you know who
I'm not bothered if he gets it, I'm nearly eighty two.

SHALL I THROW A PARTY

Shall I throw a party
I wondered to myself
I'll invite my friends and neighbours
While I'm still in good health

Shall I invite old Albert
I haven't spoke to him in years
But a party's meant for laughter
Not for shedding tears

I won't invite old Maureen
She really is a bore
I don't think she'll have changed that much
Since nineteen eighty four

I wonder whether Gloria
Would tone her make-up down
I won't invite her either
She reminds me of a clown

Oh! I know, there's big Beryl
From number thirty two
Mind you that's a bad idea
She eats enough for two

There's always dear old Ernest
And his wealthy brother Bob
Since he came into money
He's become a wealthy snob

Things aint what they use to be
I've come to realise
My family, friends and neighbours
Have changed before my eyes

So I'll just put my feet up
With a lovely cup of tea
And think of all the good times
And how things used to be

My idea to throw a party
Didn't work out right
So I'll just put the kettle on and wait for MY invite

NUMBERS

I like to play a number game
I find it so much fun
There seems to be a problem
I keep getting twenty one

Take seventeen then plus four
Or twenty then plus one
Whichever way I add it up
It comes to twenty one

So then I took a five and six
And then I added ten
And got the same old answer
Twenty one again

So I started off with forty two
And deducted twenty one
And ended up with just the same
The answer twenty one

So then I had another go
And started off with three
Then added nine plus eight
Then added one for me

I added them all up again
The answer was the same
I think you know the answer was

Twenty one again!!!

THE 1960's

When each and every ice cream was Lyon's Maid or Walls

Sour Grapes and Liquorice, Apple Tarts and Aniseed balls

Money back on bottles of Corona lemonade

Summers that were really hot

A picnic in the shade

Jubblies and The Beezer, the Beano, Desperate Dan

The Dandy and the Topper, the scary bogeyman

Pantomimes at Christmas, the throwing of the sweets

When threepenny bits and tanners were handed out as treats

One present each at Christmas

The lighting of the pud

Programmes on the tele and everyone was good

Aztec bars and Spangles

Pear Drops, Spanish Gold

When people over forty looked really, really old

Black Jacks and Fruit Salads

Sasparilla, Ginger Beer

Bazuka Joes and football cards

A clip around the ear

A Five Boys chocolate cream bar

Smarties in a box

A story when it's bedtime

Three Bears and Goldilocks

Heavy snow each Christmas, a snowman in the yard

When bin men smiled and said hello

When their job was twice as hard

So take me back to the sixties when everybody cared

About helping next door neighbours

When a problem could be shared

When our country was respected by all from overseas

But now our once Great Britain has fallen to it's knees.

TEARS OF A CLOWN

He walks through the door with a well travelled case
The lights round the mirror reflect pain in his face
He puts on his trousers four sizes too big
And hides his grey hair with a bright coloured wig

It's his final performance of thousands he's made
As the curtain comes down the limelight will fade
As he puts on the greasepaint it helps to disguise
The age in his face and the pain in his eyes

As he enters the ring of the circus once more
Amidst the applause and the familiar roar
He's everyones fool but just for a while
As he leaves to applause he portrays a big smile

Heading back to his room he savours the joy
Of being a fool since he was a boy
He takes off his costume, puts it back in his case
And removes all the greasepaint from his weathered old face

He closes the door as he turns off the light
Shuffling his feet he escapes into the night
He turns up his collar, turns his head with a frown
But nobody sees the tears of a clown

THE OLD COLLIERY BOYS

Cast your mind back to coal in a sack
When the colliers kept Britain aglow
Our country was fine when we worked down the mine
A good many years ago

What did she do, the one that wore blue
She split families causing many divorce
A working man's right is to stand up and fight
And believe in himself and his cause

Fathers and sons were at war without guns
And don't speak to this very day
She took us to task, when all we would ask
Was a days work for a decent day's pay

In our personal conquest, there was many an arrest
Of decent and proud family men
Who laid down their lives only trying to survive
And provide for their families again

It's now thirty years, it still brings me to tears
I still remember the families at war
She took all we had, turned good into bad
I thank God that she is no more

As I sit in my chair I occasionally stare
At my helmet and dusty old boots
What my life was like then, when we fought Maggie's den
But I'll always remember my roots

Now I walk hand in hand with my wife near the land
Where once was a deafening noise
And one thing's for sure, that woman's no more
I salute you, the old colliery boys.

THE HURRICANE

In a dim lit old club
Or a seedy old pub
You'd find him sat by the bar
Many don't believe what this man has achieved
Who was once Ireland's bright star

His eyes were aglaze
As he stared at the baize
Thinking of how life used to be
He was just about able to walk to the table
As he pointed his finger at me

He said "set them up
You're just a young pup
I'll teach you a lesson or two"
A smile on his face as he opened his case
And produced a battered old cue

He said "you can break
Is there a tenner at stake?"
He looked as I nodded my head
I'd hardly stepped back and in went the black
Followed by a long potted red

I stood by the bar
And watched from afar
As the guy potted ball after ball
With his chin on the cue, the crowd suddenly grew
He'd silenced the old snooker hall

Before he stepped back,
In dropped the black
And he sat down and sipped at his beer
The crowd gathered round as I gave him ten pound
And they gave him a deafening cheer

He said "listen, my son
I'm just having fun
I picked you 'cos you're cocky and vain.
You've been put in your place, remember my face
I'm Alex, the great hurricane".

FLOWERS

As the flowers start wilting on my grave
Remember all the memories we made
Like how we used to laugh
Making foam in the bath
And all the love and laughter we gave

When the grass starts to grow where I lay
I know we'll meet again another day
Please don't be sad
Remember times we had
In your memories they'll never fade away

As the leaves turn brown in Autumn years
Smile and wipe away the tears
You know I won't be far
I'll be drinking at the bar
So have a glass for me and whisper Cheers

WHY ?

Why put a man on the moon
Is this not a little too soon
When the place of our birth
Our own planet Earth
Needs attention, unlike the moon

Why put a lion in a cage
Just to tease him amused by his rage
Then set him free
And shoot as he flees
And sell the picture to a newspaper page

M P s do you think this is fun
To supply a young man with a gun
Then send him to fight
For a meaningless plight
And consider your job to be done

As you sit on your political fences
While claiming your shameful expenses
Just stop for a while
And walk for a mile
In the shoes of the boys in the trenches

THE LONG GOODBYE

Where did you go to my love
You didn't say " Goodbye"
I show you snaps of yesterday
And all you do is sigh

Are you somewhere locked away
And you hold the only key?
Hold my hand, give me a sign
That you still remember me

Sometimes your eyes will sparkle
You'll smile like years ago
But something tells me in my heart
It's time to let you go

Side by side for many years
I've loved you every day
You loved me and protected me
More than words can say

So Farewell, Goodbye my darling
We'll meet again someday
My love for you will carry on
In my heart you'll always stay.

FORGOTTEN

I've spent all my life in the forces
Altogether 35 years
I've seen it all
Young men fight and fall
As their comrades wiped away tears

When I look back at my time in Iraq
Northen Ireland and Afghanistan
Where I lived through my fears
Shed a million tears
For my comrades who never came back

Now as I sit here sipping a beer,
On a bench, straight from a can
Holding back tears
When I think of my fears
In Iraq and Afghanistan

After giving my life to my country
Have you forgotten all I have done
I have medals to show
Are you interested- no
In a veteran that once used a gun

Maybe next time you see an old soldier like me
Sat alone sipping beer on a bench
Stop for a while
Give him a smile
And say thanks for his time in the trench

THE BALLAD OF RONNIE DREW

Here's to you, Ronnie Drew
As we raise a glass, maybe two
We were all mesmorised
With a voice you can't buy.
So long to ya man, Ronnie Drew

You still light up the bars
As you sleep with the stars
With the voice you were given from God
What enjoyment you gave, we have memories to save,
Sure it's better than working the hod

From Dublin to Belfast
From Paris to Rome
Your voice was loved in all lands
At each venue you'd play they would ask you to stay
You'd return by popular demand

So Ronnie Drew, we'll meet again
When I'm laid in my box on my back
Tune your guitar and open the bar
I'll be there to have one last craic

So rest in peace Ronnie Drew
As I'm thinking of you and can hardly hold back the tears
Sing one last song, sure it won't take you long
I was one of McAlpine's Fusiliers

THE ROMANY

I said hello to the Roma man
As he passed by in his caravan

With no clue of where he's heading
Unsure of where he's been
He only dreams of clear blue sky
And a grass that's evergreen

He'll invite you to his table
To share his bread with you
And tell you tales of his travelling life
As he stirs a Joe Grey stew

We ate and laughed together
Until the night time fell
Then looked each other in the eye
And wished each other well

I thanked him for his kindness
And the stories of his life
Of how he raised his children
And how much he loved his wife

I often think about him
And how his life has been
I hope the sky stays blue for him
And the grass stays evergreen

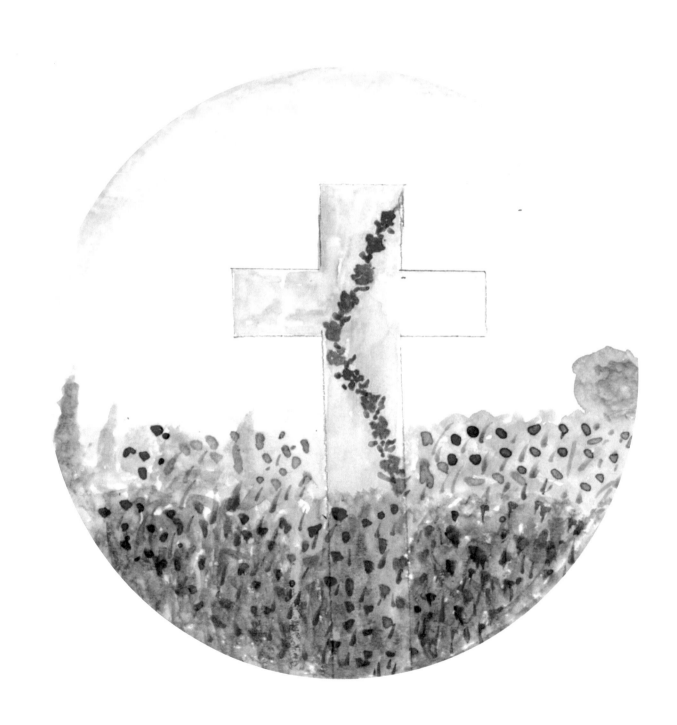

TEN THOUSAND CONCRETE SOLDIERS

Ten thousand concrete soldiers
Standing side by side
No eyes to see no mouths to speak
All stood erect with pride

Ten thousand concrete soldiers
Young men who once were free
Who sacrificed their lives for us
So Britain could be free

Ten thousand concrete soldiers
In all weathers can be seen
Their names replaced by numbers
Stood proud in fields of green

Ten thousand concrete soldiers
Just boys and barely men
Who each and every one believed
They'd come back home again

Ten thousand concrete soldiers
Stand proud with no regret
Ten thousand concrete soldiers
Lest we all forget

A BOY OF SEVENTEEN

At seventeen and just a boy I signed my life away
To represent my country in lands so far away
They put me in a uniform, the colour khaki green
And promised me I'd see the world of places never seen

They boarded us onto the ship like cattle on a farm
They said we'd grow from boys to men and never meet with harm
The ship set sail, we saluted, to family, friends and all
Who were lined up on the harbour against the grey stone wall

I turned my head and glancing up towards the dark, grey skies
Looking back towards my homeland as tears welled in my eyes
The Captain turned towards us with a reassuring stare
We headed out to meet our fate as the breeze blew through our hair

We reached our destination, the doors opened with a burst
We were led like lambs to slaughter, the date July the first
The boys who charged in front of us were blown to smithereens
We lost a lot of boys that day, barely in their teens

As years go by I wonder if I'd have changed that fateful day
The day I signed the papers and gave my life away
In my lapel I wear a poppy and wear it with such pride
To show that I remember the thousands that had died

The red for blood, the black for death, the green that says we're free
And the heroes and the lucky ones that survived it all like me
So always buy a poppy to sit in your lapel
To remind you of our heroes and all the boys that fell

WASTED LAND

As I headed down a pathway on a beaten down old track
I thought I'd stop and rest a while to ease my aching back
While resting on a wooden bench and gazing out to sea
Memories of yester year came flooding back to me

No more children's laughter just dunes of whispering sand
The putt putt of motor boats and Morris dancing bands
No astroglide or go-carts, arcades and cafe's gone
Just a derelict mass of wasteland discoloured by the sun

I know you can't stop progress, I wouldn't want to try
But looking down on wasteland a tear welled in my eye
Turning back and heading home and asking myself why?
A paradise for children should fade away and die

So at the next election Mums and Dads take note
Be very very careful to whom you give your vote
The councillors who rang your bell you never see again
They're busy on another line or on holiday in Spain

So if you go out walking and gaze out to the sea
You may stumble upon some wasteland and reminisce like me
Of happy days, of years gone by and fun in summer weather
Stop and rest and think a while, but nothing lasts forever

19 66

30 July 1966

As he led his lions on to the pitch
Amidst the Wembley roar
Ball in hand to lead his side
The legend Bobby Moore

Banks and Styles behind him
Wilson, Cohen, Ball
Every English legend
So proud and walking tall

Bobby and his brother
Peters, Hunt and Hurst
As every street was empty
The ground about to burst

Some still this day will argue
If the ball did cross that line
But we knew that we were champions
They were only wasting time

The Germans made their exit
Bodies stooped, their heads were bowed
Amidst the celebrations
And the cheering of the crowd

Some people ran on to the pitch
But there was one last kick
Our number ten Sir Geoff Hurst
Completed his hat trick
We knew it was all over
Lift the cup and take a bow
We never will forget that day
It's truly over now

Mr JONES

He taught when to listen
And when to hold my tongue
He told me to apologise
When you realise you are wrong

He taught me how to show respect
To your elders when you can
And always give a helping hand
To the more unfortunate man

He said to me - You'll be allright
Don't worry what's out there
Make sure you always clean your shoes
And always comb your hair

He said to me - It's impossible
To learn experience in a day
And when your peers are talking
Don't turn your head away

He said to me - Now listen, son
If you want to go quite far
Stay away from alcohol
And leaning on a bar

He said - I'm far from perfect
But please take my advice
Mistakes will only happen once
But a habit happens twice

So I've tried to listen to his words
That chilled me to my bones
I never will forget you
And thank you, Mr Jones

RIP JAY

JAMES AND LEE

Memories stay forever
Of the laughter, fun and tales
When two young lads from Kirkby
Came to sunny Wales
The motor boats, the astroglide
The laughter in the sun
A pocketful of pennies
Times of priceless fun

The bang on old machines
Did no-one any harm
As we'd run away with laughter
To the sound of loud alarms
Swimming in the Nova
Bombing in the pools
Ejected in the afternoon
For breaking all the rules

As years go by and time moves on
Those buildings have all gone
Just echoes of the laughter
Of times of having fun
They say that time's a healer
But sadly not for me
There will always be an empty space
Where your laughter used to be

To people whom you met through life
You've left a heavy heart
But for us who really knew you
We'll never be apart
So until we meet again, Jay
Wherever you may be
Thank you for the memories
Of how we used to be